T

Witches Night Out

Spell Book

'I don't believe in magic.'
The young boy said.
The old man smiled.
'You will, when you see her.'

First Edition
First Printing, 2017

The Witches Night Out Spell Book/ Deb Stratton
The Witches Night Out Spell Book is in no way affiliated with the WNO organization.

ISBN-13: 978-1974512676

ISBN-10: 1974512673

ThornDove Publications

Printed in the United States Of America

Dedication:

To all of the amazing and powerful women I have met along my journey.

It has been a privilege and a blessing to have you all as a part of my life.

My mom

Jessica, Shelby, Emily my trio of beauty
Dawn S. My sweet southern friend
Diane P. My true Salem Witch
Pam W. "Somebody that I used to know"
My sisters Jenny & Bridget
My Grandma Clark & Aunt Jackie

"Wherever crows are, there is magic"

We all have a little witch in us, some more than others. Each day is a new chance to create your own magic.

As the season of the harvest and the witch continues during our favorite month of the year. October.

Put on your witch hat and look at the moon. Break out your Spell Book and spank your Baboon.

Well not really, don't do that. Just cast a spell and get witchy.

"All of the great stories have witches in them"

*Introduction

A lifelong love for witches and all things magical has led to the making of this book. When I was young I found myself dreaming of many things in life and one of them was...well magic!

I love the idea of conjuring up some good luck spell and sitting under the full moon. I have enjoyed watching and rewatching all of those movies that portray the mysterious life of the covens and witches as well.

The word magic had been used to describe many different practices. From simple spells, to healing, fortune telling and much more.

This book is just for fun but it is filled with some great spells, crafts and more!

"Always throw spilled salt over your shoulder. Keep rosemary by your garden gate. Add pepper to your mashed potatoes. Plant roses and lavender for luck. FALL IN LOVE whenever you can."

Table of Contents

Chapter One

Magic Crafts & Photo's

The symbolism of the mirror is simple and complex. Mirrors allow us to see things we could not without their aid. Not only physical but glimpses of the future, memories and visions.

Find a mirror, wash it, cool before use. Cover the mirror with a black cloth and do not use until the full moon. On that night, expose your mirror to the moonlight. Charge the mirror with the moonlight. Keep your mirror on an eastern wall. Keep it covered when not in use.

Write your ideas here!

Witchy Crafts

One of my favorite crafts to make over the years has been silverware windchimes. You may have seen them dangling from a limb in a movie scene. In the movie Practical Magic I noticed several hanging in one tree. It was the first time that I had seen them hung in a movie that displayed their true meaning.

So gather up your old silverware and make yourself one or two. They make great gifts.

Silverware Windchimes

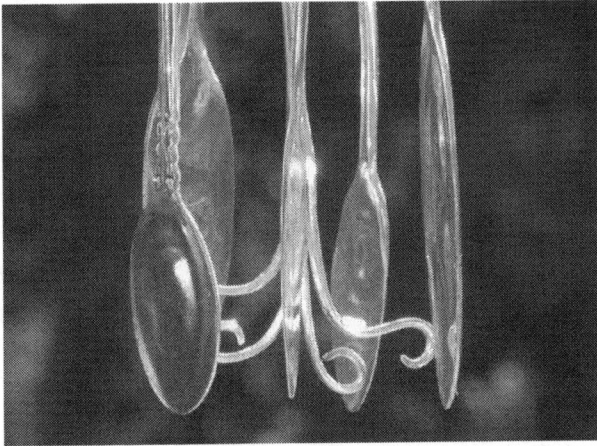

First: Pound out all of your forks and spoons with a hammer. You will want to wrap them in an old towel to keep from damaging them. Place them on a sidewalk or hard surface to do this.

Second: Use a hand drill or drill press to drill holes in the ends of the silverware. Thread fishing line through the holes and attach to the top. I usually bend one fork apart in 4 directions to use for the main hanger and then add the additional silverware to each of the prongs. They will dangle very nicely. The wind will keep your home and property safe

from all wrong doers.

More silverware facts:

If you drop a fork a man will soon come visit.
If you drop a spoon a woman will knock on the door.

If two forks are laid next to your plate without a
knife you will be invited to a wedding.

It's all about the Broom

A besom is a broom. Call it a must have household implement used for sweeping. The term is now mostly reserved for a traditional broom constructed from a bundle of twigs tied to a stout pole.

The broom is used to cleanse and purify a space which will be used for ritual. A traditional Wiccan besom has a hawthorne stave handle with bristles made from birch twigs. These twigs are tied on using thin pieces of willow wood. Hawthorne is one of my most favorite woods to work with. I did not use willow to tie my broom up, I used grapevine pieces.

It is used to cleanse the ritual area. While it does not usually touch the ground, it is used to "sweep out" the negative energies in a room, and is often held a few inches above the ground to do so.

How to make it:

I spent the day gathering sticks and twigs in the woods. If you do not have a large yard or a lot of trees you can go to a local park and take a walk. This works best because of the variety. Most of the handles that I have made were from fallen tree limbs. They are already dried perfectly and look very rustic and witchy.

Gather the sticks up and make sure they are all about 2 feet long. I have made longer ones and they look much better as a porch broom. After gathering use some jute twine to tie around the top to bunch it up. This is just to get a look at how it will appear after attaching to the handle. If you like the design go ahead and place the broom handle down into the middle of the large bunch of sticks and tie the twine around to secure it in place. I use the twine under the grapevine twists to keep it from falling apart.

You can use colored thread or twine if you would like to give the broom some color. What are you waiting for? Lets hit the woods and make one!

The Cauldron

Used to brew and hold potions. Cauldrons are usually heated over an open fire.

Using one outside during the fall months is one of my favorite things to do! Hanging one is difficult if using cast iron. Look for strong tree branches or build one out smaller tree trunks.

Double, Double
Toil and Trouble

Fireburn
And
Cauldron Bubble

What is the story behind the Cauldron?

A Cauldron in general is a large pot for cooking over an open fire. Most caldrons have an arch shaped handle used to hang it with. Traditionally they were made from cast iron and rest on three legs.

Witches throughout history had used them to cook up potions and spells.

"Dust off your hats and brooms and throw on your best
"Witchy Wear" Join us for a spell out on the town!

An amazing photo of an Antique Witch

"Bewitched...Bewitched... By far one of my most favorite shows and the movie was just as wonderful to me.

"Witches Honor"

Yes... you should color this
beautiful spider

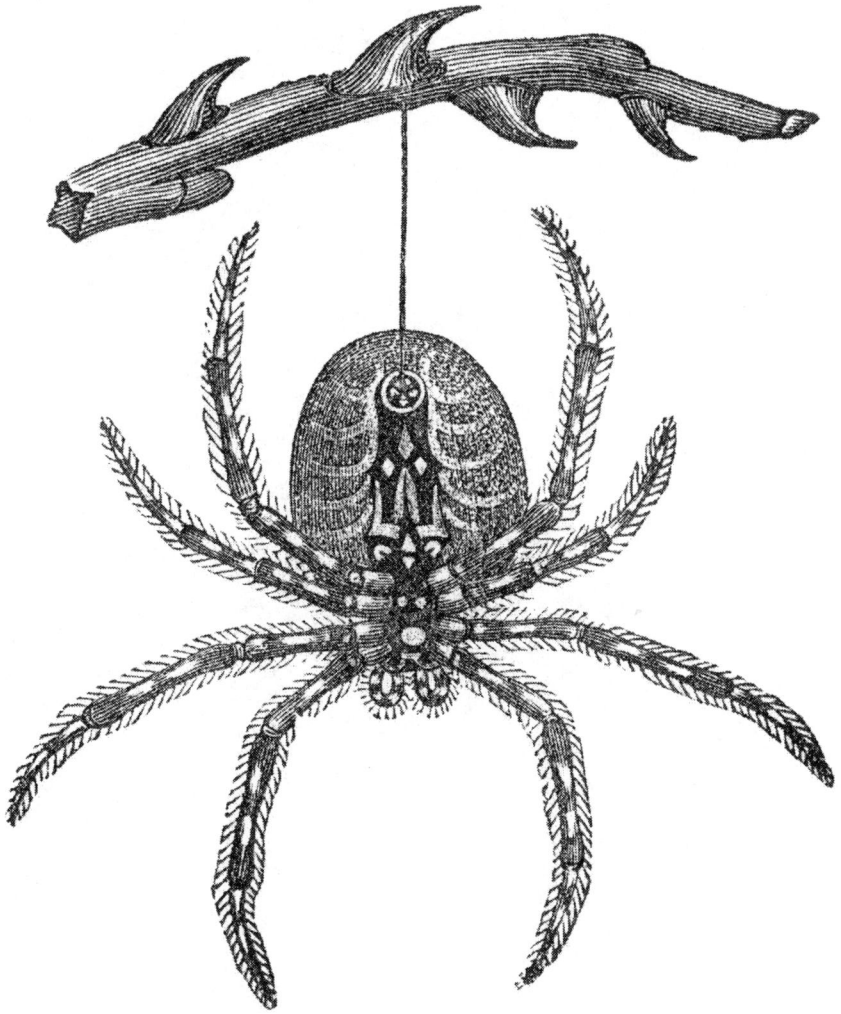

And you can color this also!
Beautiful!

Chapter Two

Superstitions & Folklore

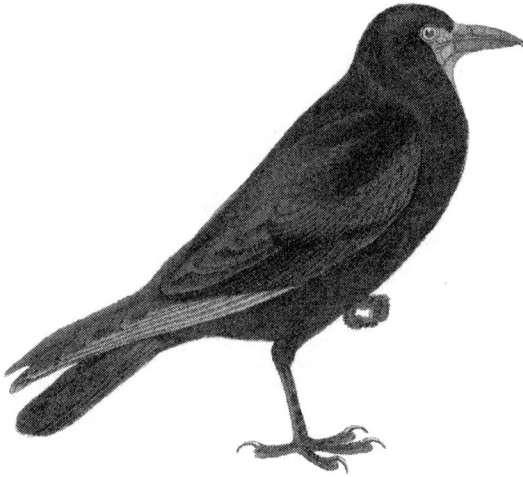

Birds have a history of being associated with witches. Very similar to the way witches have been able to fly in history on their brooms.

Birds have been said to be natural messengers. Some birds bring good luck, bird droppings can bring very good luck and birds landing on you can bring good fortune and fame.

There are many superstitions regarding birds. Birds hitting the glass on the windows of your home can indicate a baby is coming.

Birds coming into the house can indicate a more dreadful outcome.

Certain types of birds also have other meanings. A rooster crowing at night can be a warning of bad news.

Hearing or seeing doves on your wedding day indicates happiness, however, if you hear a rooster on that day it can indicate a short marriage.

Typically seen with witches are crows or ravens. The black birds seem to flock around all things magic. The birds themselves are very smart and wise.

There are also many superstitions that involve these types of birds.

A crow seen in the middle of the road is a sign of a happy and safe journey. Seeing only one crow would indicate sadness and seeing two would bring joy.

The sign of a dead crow is to return home. Seeing one in the road in this fashion would mean to turn around and not take the trip you were going on.

Swallows are a good luck bird. Having these types of birds near your home is a sign of good luck. It has also been told that harming these birds or their nests will bring sadness and bad luck.

Owls are so majestic and wise. To harm this bird is considered the worst of luck possible. They are considered a bad omen just by seeing them. Take caution.

Robins are a good sign if you are buying property. Magpies are good luck if seen together. Seeing or hearing only one near you can indicate a crime or theft on its way.

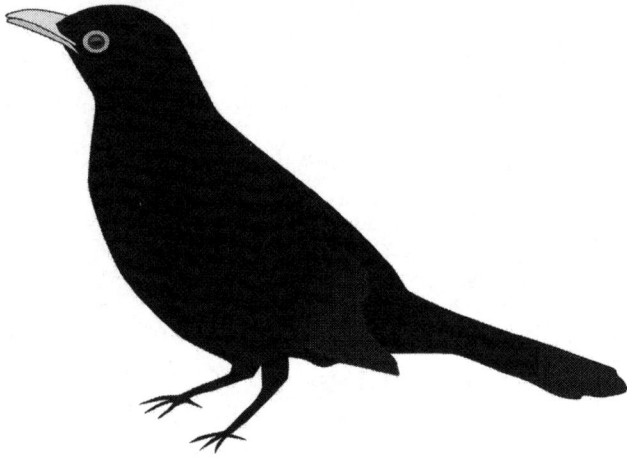

It is good luck if a blackbird makes a nest on your house.

If you see 5 crows, sickness will follow; see 6 crows and death will follow.

To avoid bad luck tip your hat if you see a magpie.

Whatever you do to a robin will happen to you, so be nice!

It is bad luck to see an owl during the day.

A kingfisher is a very lucky bird.

Three seagulls flying together, directly overhead, are a warning of death soon to come.

Sparrows carry the souls of the dead, it's unlucky to kill one.

When a swan lays its head and neck back over its body during the daytime it means a storm is coming.

Having a wren around will prevent one from drowning. A bird that flies into a house foretells an important message. However, if the bird dies, or is white, this foretells death.

"FIND A PENNY, PICK IT UP.

ALL DAY LONG, YOU'LL HAVE GOOD LUCK."

This common rhyme refers to an old superstition, and like many superstitions, it has many variations and the reasoning behind those variations are also numerous. Reasons why finding pennies brings good luck range from early beliefs about where metal came from to the notion that money symbolizes power.

Bad things can happen to good people when they least expect it. As a result, people tend to fall back on ancient rituals that seem to stave off disaster. That is, they believe in superstitions. Many superstitions seem to revolve around the struggle between good and evil, and these rituals were designed to swing the balance onto the side of good.

"Only pick up a penny that is heads up, put it in your shoe for luck."

"Never cross the path of a black cat"

Chapter Three

Spells

Are you ready?

You are motivated, determined and ready to try a spell but don't know where to start? Spellcasting can be as easy or as difficult as you want it to be. It can be simple or complex. It can be mental or emotional or both. It can also be physical and spiritual. It can include as many or as little ingredients and tools as you'd like. The options are endless and are all up to you.

What is a spell, exactly? A spell is focused intention and harnessed energy. Spells can be used for personal gain, as we are in control of our own lives and where we go in life. They should not be used to gain control over others, however. But ultimately morals are at the behest of the spellcaster, and so the individual will deal with the consequences.

For those who feel the need to have a spell already written for you, and one that is easy to follow and perform, check out the easy spells on the pages that follow to help get you started. Feel free to modify them to your needs!

The Send Back Spell

Whenever you feel that bad thoughts are being sent in your direction from known or unknown persons, this spell can be utilized. Before it set a white candle, be careful not to let it reflect in the mirror. Stand before the mirror and light a match. As you light the white candle think of sending back any bad energy that has been sent your way. See it leaving you and returning to the sender. Repeat this for a few moments and leave the room. After one hour snuff out the candle and put the mirror away. Repeat the spell for 7 nights.

There are many spells that include the use of a wall mirror or handheld. Some may use a small makeup mirror that you can keep with you in times of need.

Knot Your Troubles Away

You can use this one no matter what your problem is. If you choose a color for the yarn to suit your purpose, you can fine-tune the spell to your particular situation. All you need for this spell is a piece of yarn in the appropriate color, at least 12 inches long.

Now hold the yarn, with one end in each hand and pull it taut. Think about your problem (just one per spell, please). Concentrate on your difficult situation and start tying knots in the yarn. Visualize all your troubles getting bound up in the knots and trapped there. Tie the knots until you feel it's enough.

Take the knotted yarn outside and bury it to keep your problems away.

A Sprinkling of Protection

Keep your house safe and sound with a little protection magic. Of course, that doesn't mean you should leave your door unlocked either. Common sense works well with magick. You will need:

- A handful of salt
- A teaspoon or so of garlic powder

A FULL MOON

You will not be able to use pre-made garlic salt. Mix the salt and garlic together, and sprinkle a little bit of it at each door threshold and windowsill. It will help keep out negative energy.

Wish Spell

"May the Goddess and God
of light and love,
grant me my wish
and quiet my heart.
I place my desire in your hands,
For you to do as you will
and as I deserve.
So mote it be."

The most common spells that I have used are protection spells. Going back to the act of hanging the silverware windchimes in tree to placing onions in the corners of your house.

Feeling safe and protected creates peace. Living a life filled with peace, happiness and love is the greatest goal of any good witch.

des ni oibg tnis sibon setncidebo
℣ Jesum ✝ tum Filium tuum
atque ♏ Παεχκλγίον Amen.

Citatio.

Ego N.N. otic & οϲου et mepicnirp
♏ NN. ut jam mihi appareas in
specie humana celeriter et citatim
℣ Nn Ineffabile יהוה Creatoris ōu
♈ ℣ & ♍ ⊕i, Angelos Ms ♏ ♈ Γ
♉ & □a q̃ ✝a sunt in ☉ & ☽ prae
cipio vobis ut ihim muruaoeht
♈ ♈ ♄ ☉ ♈ ⚊⚊⚊ extrahas ostendas
et tradas in Nē ♌ Bathat vel vachat
Suꝑ Abrac ruens supvenienseñocor
Suꝑ Aberer, advenias hucusque
hactenus horsam ante huncce
muluerie in quo sum jam in ♐

4 ☉ ☿ ♀ ☽

Protinus, continuo, tantumodo,
fac Tu quod volo abs Te et Ego
vicißim faciam quod Hanorem

Chapter Four

Fortune Telling

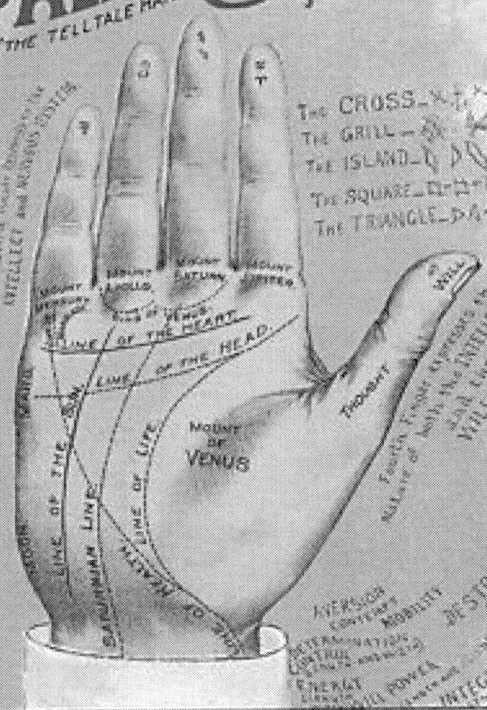

Palm Readings

I have always loved the art of reading Palms. Go ahead show me your hand. I can look for just a moment and tell you about your relationships. I may be able to see how many children you will have. The palm has very obvious markings that describe your temper, personality, work, life, health and so much more.

In addition to reading your future the lines can also identify if you have low levels of vitamins in your body. I can also see if you drink too much caffeine. Isn't that crazy? It is all there right in front of you.

I always read the right hand. There are many different readers out there and many have learned from older family members that developed what worked for them.

I believe that the right hand is your future and current life. The left hand is what you would have done with your life but never will.

Your left hand may show different careers, marriages and even the number of children. The right hand is always correct in my readings.

One of my favorite markings on the hands is in the center of the palm. I have been too several events for readings and if your are adorned with an "X" it is an indicator of psychic intuition. It is very prominent on most mediums and psychics that you encounter. Take a look. Do you have one?

Look again. Is there a triangle? That is a sign of health protection. Some people have multiple.

My tent at the Witches Night Out this year is focusing on palm reading. I am excited to see what it brings!

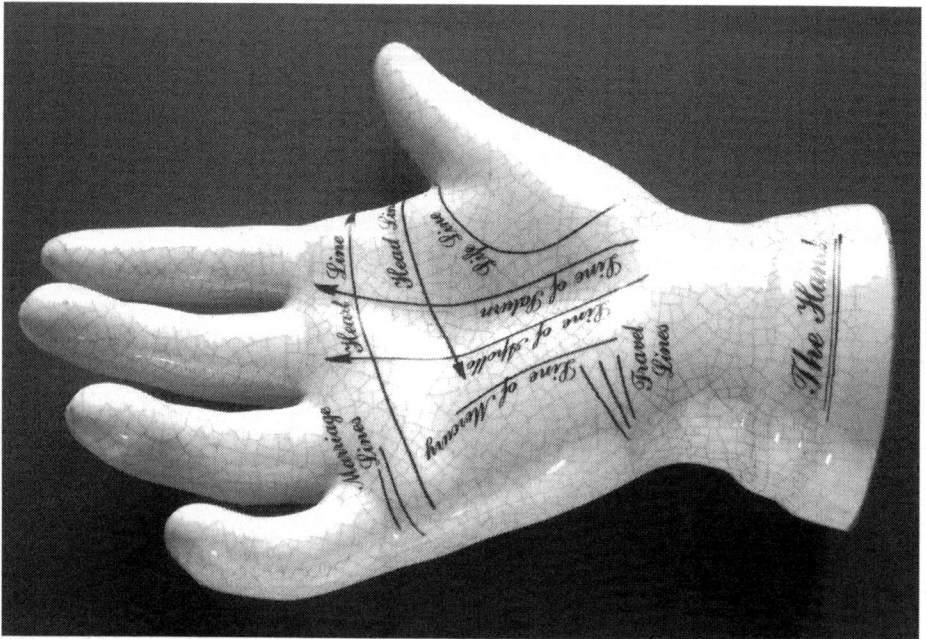

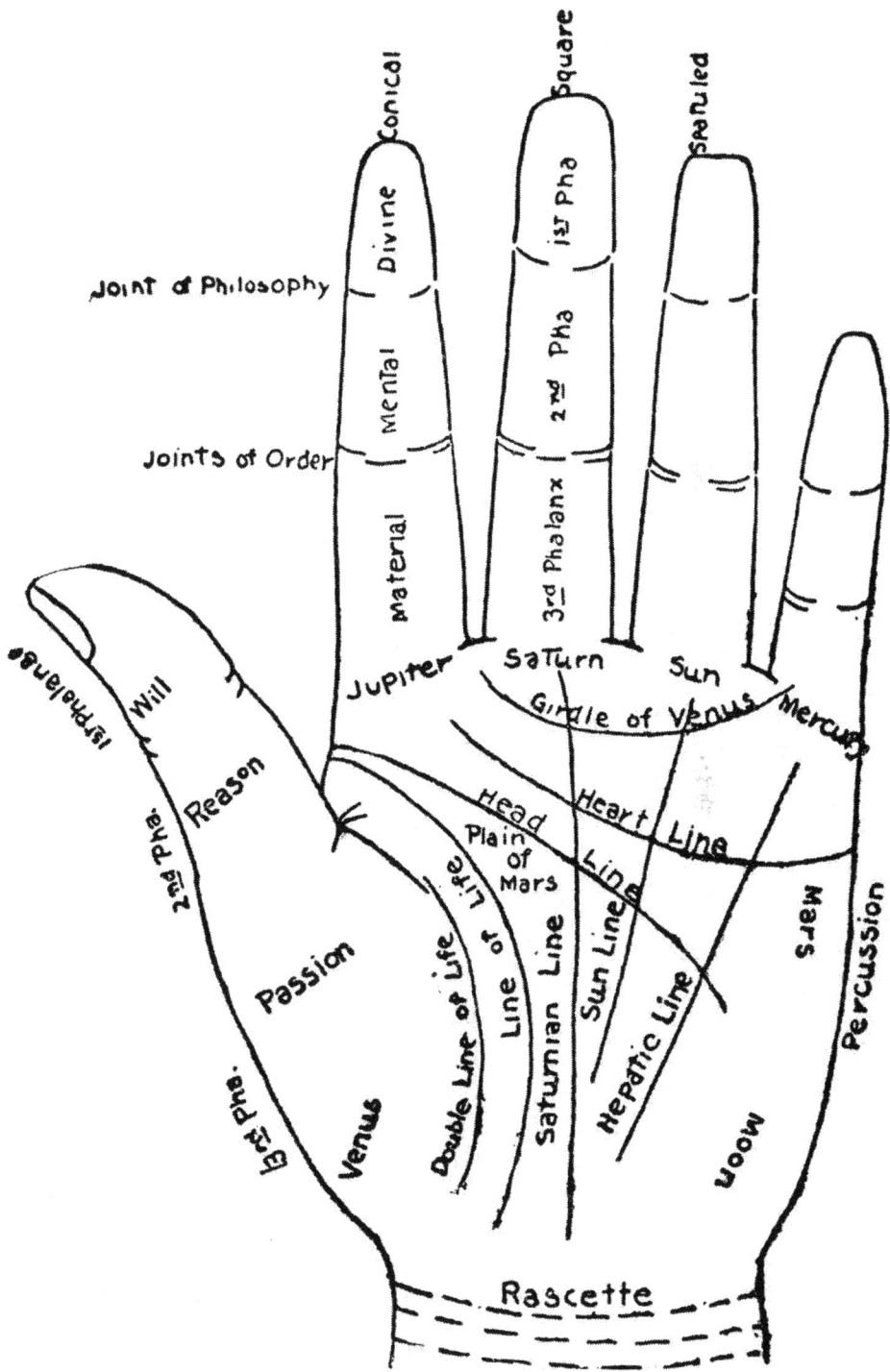

Tarot Card Readings

I have had a large collection of cards for many years. The artwork and variety is amazing. My favorite to use for many years was the Rider Tarot Deck, that changed a few years ago after my daughter found an old deck under the floorboard in the house. The old floor had a loose board and what a surprise to find such a treasure.

The discovered cards were amazing to use. Large and full of energy. They have proven to provide the very best readings around.

The Tarot deck is made up of 78 Tarot cards, each with its own unique Tarot card meaning. There are 22 Major Arcana cards and 56 Minor Arcana cards across four suits (Cups, Pentacles, Swords and Wands).

The Major Arcana consists of 22 cards that reflect key archetypes or spiritual lessons in our lives.

The Minor Arcana consists for four suits—Cups, Pentacles, Swords, and Wands. Each of these suits contains 14 cards, which reflect the day-to-day activities in our lives.

ιe Major Arcana Tarot cards form the
ιation of the Tarot deck. The deck consists of
twenty-one numbered cards and one unnumbered
card (the Fool).

These cards represent a path to spiritual
awareness and indicate the greater meaning and
understanding. In this way, they hold deeply
meaningful lessons.

The Major Arcana Tarot card meanings illustrate
the structure of human consciousness and hold the
keys to life lessons passed down through the ages.

Tarot card spreads are usually chosen depending
on the questions or circumstances of the questioner
(or the person having the reading).

I usually try to stay away from the past, present
and future spread for multiple reasons. One, the
questioner knows the past. It is not usually the
reason for the reading. However, it can help me
understand what the future cards mean.

Using this spread has never really helped too
many people. That is just my opinion. I have seen
many readers use it with success.

I use a 5 or 7 card spread for most readings.
The center card is my main focus and it gives me
insight on a major life event or issue. The cards

surrounding it will always fall into place. They offer insight into other areas that complete the reading. It is mostly like fitting puzzle pieces together.

Tarot card readings are best in person. By having the questioner touch the cards and provide information about their questions or concerns, the reading is much more helpful.

I have done readings over the phone for psychics that have called me due to not being able to read their own cards. This is very common. A lot of tarot card readers do not read their own cards.

I have read my own a few times and have not really been too impressed with my results.

In the past few years I have also been asked to read cards regarding cases of a missing person. Reading cards for a questioner that is needing information on someone missing can be very difficult but also very accurate. I have been correct every single time I have done this. That is an amazing energy to have.

I will always enjoy expanding my collection and hope that if you have chosen to have a reading with me at some point that it was helpful and filled with the hope that you needed to get you to the next journey. Tarot is filled with hope. A useful tool to help you make sense of life and things that you cannot understand on your own.

Chapter Five

Delightful Rituals & Charms

Smudging

I burn sage or a sweet grass at my home before reading cards or relaxing.

Dried white sage has a distinctly beautiful scent when burned.

You can take a moment of meditation to notice if the smell evokes a sense memory for you. Where does that resonate in your body? This is the smell of thousands of years of spiritual communion and ritual.

I recently started growing my own sage. I have collected ribbons to wrap them while drying. You can find many tutorials online for this and I will also include a photo of what they look like.
Smudging your sacred space, your home or even your body with sage is like taking an energetic shower.

It is like doing a deep metaphysical cleansing. The smoke from dried sage actually changes the ionic composition of the air, and can have a direct effect on reducing our stress response. Try it!

Sweet grass is my next favorite. Call me crazy but I had never had this or used it until I went to a barn sale in Hermann Missouri. There was a man hosting the small sale and as I pulled up he was braiding the sweet grass peacefully. I walked through his small barn and seen a braid of sweet grass on the table. I could not take my eyes off of it.

I decided to ask him about his braiding and he told the story of how sweet grass was grown in our area and how he began growing it himself. I ended up leaving with a gift that I would never forget. I loved it so much I did not want to burn it. I did decide to just a bit. That is the great thing about smudging. You do not use too much of your sticks at once and they tend to last longer than you would think.

When you get your sage stick home light it and walk around just a bit. Set it on a special dish. While it is burning call forth the energy of peace and love. This ancient mystical ritual is a simple one to incorporate into your daily or weekly routine, or any time you feel like you might need a little aura polishing. You can never really smudge too much!

Wondering when would be the best time to smudge? Try it when you move into a new home or apartment. Older homes are usually in need quickly of this. I always smudge after a visitor stops by. If you know the guest is coming you can smudge before, just remember the smell can be odd for others are first and they may give you the look. You can go ahead and cleanse again after they leave.

Other good times would include meditating, healing sessions and massage. After an illness.

After a disagreement or argument with someone. After returning home from work or crowded places.

Once you have a nice smoke going, use your hand or a feather to direct the smoke over your body from your feet up to your head, then back down again. As you do this, visualize the smoke taking away with it negative energy.

Peacefully chant these words:

"Air, fire, water, earth. Cleanse, dismiss, dispel."

I usually walk around a bit and then wave the smoke around the different areas.

Smudging

Smudging is burning herbs most commonly Sage to get rid of negative energy on yourself, your home or any space. Smudging can be useful when you're feeling depressed, angry, resentful, unwell or after you have had an argument with someone or if you have felt a negative presence in your home or you feel there are unwanted spirits. You would normally use a smudge stick to do this, you can make your own or buy them from most new age stores. Smudging is thousands of years old it was used by Native Americans, in ancient Rome and Greece and ancient Egypt as a way to cleanse a space from bad spirits and negative energy.

cedar

mugwort

To smudge, light a smudge stick and let it catch fire. Extinguish the fire and let the smoke billow from the stick. Walk around your home letting the smoke get everywhere, in every room, in cupboards and small spaces. The smoke is not dangerous and will not harm you or your pets. Use a bowl to catch any ashes.

sage

What I wouldn't do for a great sage stick.

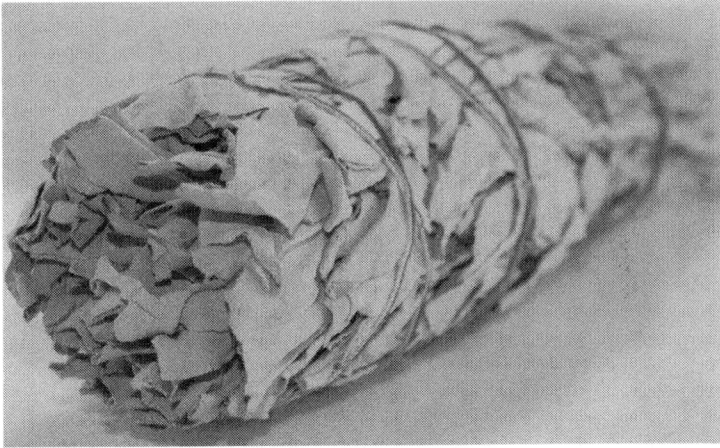

Happy Smudging!

Poppet Dolls

Poppet Dolls are used in a variety of ways in cultures across the world. They are a very common form of sympathetic magic and can be used to manifest a number of desired effects.

The protection poppet doll is for healing and protective energy. Often the dolls are filled with herbs such as lavender for bring love, peace and joy into the keepers life.

The dolls are not toys and capable of creating many desired effects. In addition to the protection dolls, you may personalize your doll to meet your main objective. Whether it be love, fertility or health.

The poppet can bring these hopes and dreams to a place of high probability.

On occasion the dolls can be confused by others as a vudu (voodoo) doll. There is a difference between the magic and energy of these dolls.

Some choose to use their poppet with scribing pins which mimic the vudu doll. The pins enforce the desire behind the spell.

The dolls are made to resemble a person in order to cast a spell on them or do harm. The use of the Vudu Doll is very different because the intent is harmful and not loving.

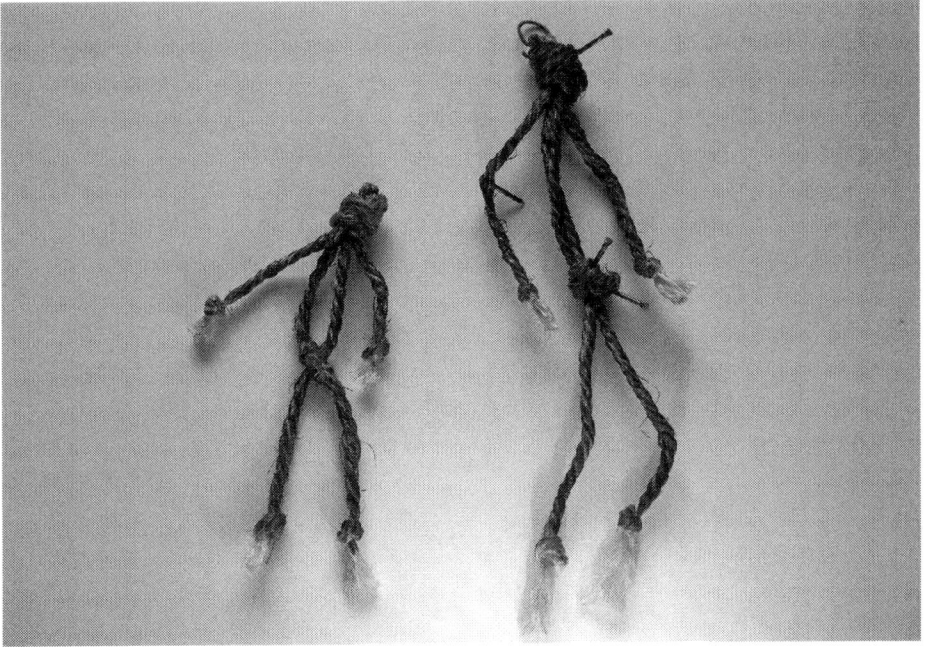

The power of Crystals and Stones

Crystal energy is the power that crystals naturally give off and that you are able to use to heal yourself.

You can apply the metaphysical properties of these more powerful crystals, as you learn how you can use them to heal yourself.

It is a great advantage to have natural crystals of any sort in your environment, and the stones with a higher vibration are powerful aids to move you forwards in your life.

Some crystals have higher frequencies, and their strong energy fields can be used to raise your personal vibration.

Create Change

Many people are drawn to high crystal energy stones at this time of extraordinary changes on the earth.

The higher vibration crystals are the primary healing stones that may be used to assist you in your spiritual healing journey.

Many of these stones have potent energy that may create quite amazing change in your life.

If they are within your auric field they will resonate with a constant high vibration energy, and this is a vibration that your body may use to heal itself.

Depending on what sort of healing you require, there are special stones that you might use for different reasons. Most of the stones of a higher vibration resonate most strongly within the chakras from the heart up.

Making a multi crystal wand allows you to use the amazing range of different crystals healing properties together, for an extraordinary healing outcome.

In Christ
month of
the muse
this trans
to see a
some oth
Kelly. Dr.
and later
crystal,
December
and the
Preface
Kelly" gav
was effec
the said
being inc
it, and A
and broug
in the ye
in the po
me the
complain
I was li
called v
many wa
use a v
of the bo
which ex
with wor
the sign
Adonai b
aricot!
on or
scenit
witnes
n the

Chapter Six

Finding Beauty in all things magical

What is more magical than finding beauty in others? Look through the pages of some very inspirational and beautiful women sharing their love for the craft.

Victoria Long

Sumter, SC

Her Loves:

"Throwing salt over your shoulder, when gifting a purse or wallet always put money inside to avoid bad financial luck. Windows should be opened in the home when someone has passed to allow the soul to leave."~ "I love smudging-cleansing homes and candles for specific routines and spells. My stones mean the world to me." "I look forward to receiving my own deck of tarot cards and learning to read."

Sandra Sue Fowler

Peoria, Illinois

The Fowler name traces back to the 1600's and is a prominent name in Salem. Generations of witches have grown throughout the family. Sandra (Sandy) the mother. Superstitions fill the air.
There are many.
A beautiful woman in and out. Her motherly love is known to many.

Bianca Gifford

Oviedo Florida
Her Love: African Witchcraft

"African Witchcraft has always been so interesting to me. Vodun, AKA voodoo, has been popular for ages and is said to originate in West Africa. To me, it's very spiritual and not as violent as others have portrayed. I feel as if voodooists have a great sense of life, their spiritual being, and death. Self-realization and self-actualization plays a big part on how people see themselves and the world. I also enjoy how these voodoo objects can be seen as a piece of art."

A trio of Witches
Jennifer, Vanessa & Rachel

The Queen of Halloween
For a true experience of the Season stroll past this house in
Saint Louis for an amazing evening filled with an unforgettable
display of all things magical.

For the past several years, Jennifer and her children Vanessa,
Rachel (featured above), Tony, Daisy and Oliver spend months
planning the perfect Halloween experience.

Superstitions:
"Never step on a crack or your break your mother's back."

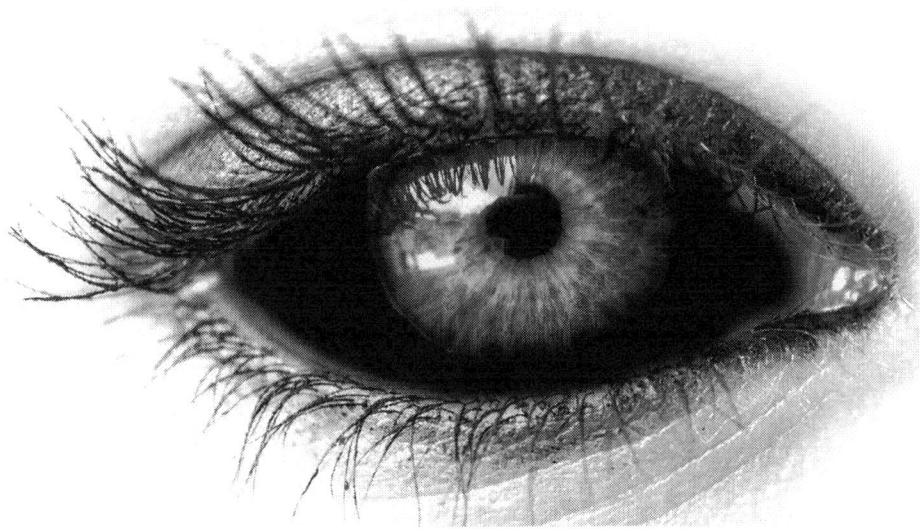

Blessed Be

Pegasus Pills

Makes you fly

Use: Take when needed
Be careful to be in
open air

Octopus Tentacles

To grow more limbs

Use: as a compress where
you want the extra limb

Scorpion's
Poision Drops

To smell good

Use: One drop on your skin
will make you smell
good for a day!

Eagle Nails

For bravery

Use: Mix two teaspoons
in your cereal

Black Spider's Hair

To blacken your hair

Use: mix with water and wash
your hair with the
mixture

Sea Horse Tails

To brew a love potion

Use: Buy the recipe for the
love potion by
The Magic Apothecary

NOTES

Bec de la figure en haut Buffon
Bill of the Figure above

N°. 145   N°. Corneau ou Corneille Noire de Buffon
english   Crow ou magpie entire blackness of the whole feathers
                                              T. Lewin

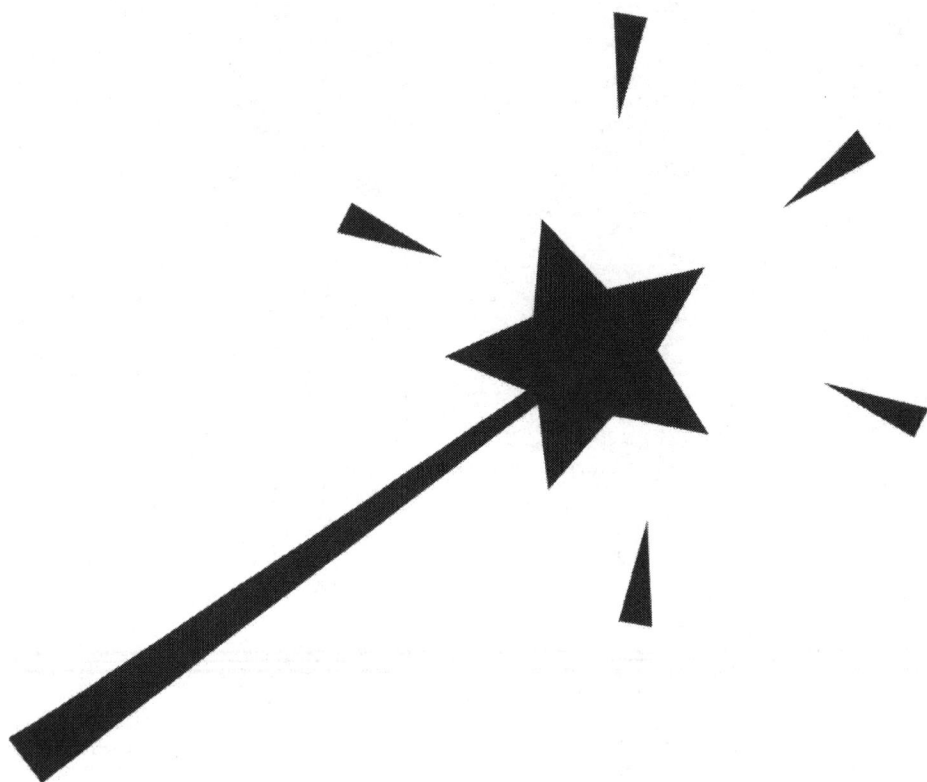

My Tarot Readings

My Palm Readings

My Psychic Readings

The End

75970373R00101

Made in the USA
Columbia, SC
29 August 2017